The Record of a Memory

Milian Chen

The Record of a Memory

A Collection of Written Poetry

Milian Chen

This book is a work of discovery and ideas, hopefully to explore the world.
A lot of care and consideration has been put into these words, and I hope they're able to resonate with you in some way.

The Record of a Memory
Copyright © 2023 by Milian Chen

First published in 2023 by WEI-WEN CHEN in Vancouver, BC, Canada
www.wmvmedia.com

Cover Photography by Milian Chen
Interior Art and Photography by Milian Chen
Back Cover Photography by Milian Chen

ISBN: 978-1-7380587-0-9 (ebook)
ISBN: 978-1-7380587-1-6 (paperback)

The text of this book is set mostly in 14 point Garamond.

To my parents,

Who braved all the waves,
Saw all that came,
And stayed with me,
Day by day

Beginnings

Poetry was a journey for me. Nursery rhymes, children's books, and fascinating novels built my roots deep into writing and expression. Some books I've kept with me for a long time, while others I've only just reunited with. While I don't remember the first stanzas or poems that I've written, I do recall eagerly producing a poem about the Sun to my mom, after I had returned from a day in second grade. It was a flurry after that, ideas here and there with other projects. When 2022-2023 came around, it was a whirlwind of idea after idea, with a hundred or so pages of drafts and finished products (I can't fathom how many poems that adds up too...)- 73 of which you get to meet in this book. This is technically my second poetry book, the first a compilation of poems written in fifth grade. A sense of nostalgia surrounds me whenever I read it, now seven years away from that version of myself. I hope I'll achieve her dreams. Poetry has been a home for me too, a place to express my ideas on paper in a safe place. Its helped me open doors into worlds in a different way than novels do, but with the same passion and intrigue. This art holds a special place in my heart (hehe, see what I did there?) and so have the experiences that led me to create them. These are little snippets of my life, a snapshot of my memory. I hope this journey treats you well, and welcome. Into my mind.

Table of Contents

Bliss

I sit here and dream

Of all the sunsets I miss

Every day that goes round

How can I feel bliss?

To just sit there and stare

At the sun and it's glare

As it softens to pastels

I can look on, say farewell

As the clouds dance and twirl

Their shapes changing and winds shrill

There's comfort in the cold air

Nothing I could find elsewhere

When the Sky Falls

The sun rising at a distance

Closing the worlds of dark and light

Surrounding me

What could cause me to look up

From this upside down world

Rise into strength

Frown at thoughts

Sights gone and hearing lost

Voices drowned and tasteless

Blue streaks

I look up at the sky

Long Ago

Forest mist makes me misty eyed

When it reminds me of long ago

When there were castles and kings

Palaces and queens

And dainty blood on snow

The Water Breaks

when the world tumbles at the edges

and you struggle to get up

let the waves crash against your back

bite back the pain in your heart

kneel forward and fall back

into the fields and into the light

maybe, maybe, this is right

Little Pieces of Me

Diamonds in the rough

Instrumentals in the background

Last pages of a book

Through every nook and cranny you'll find

The little pieces of me

My fantasy, my dream

The truth behind the curtain walls

The faith through these majestic halls

The Tiger

Behind the walls

A tiger purrs and prowls

Past the silken sheets and emptied halls

The stealthily placed paws

Not a trace is left behind

Rabbit on a Mission

Long ears flop as the rabbit hops

Down and down the lane

To every house with reddened panes

It sees the lanterns glow

Spreading all around to show

What warmth this winter can bring

Leaving little footprints, round and small

Giving happiness and luck to all

Pearl Teardrops

Iridescent reflections

Inner-world remembrance

Rivers of guilt and fear

Waterfalls pouring at the brim

Moonstones gleam under sunlight

Pearls strung against a tree

Neck adorned with thorns

Treasures of the sea

Presents of the ocean

Mirror made of sea glass

Washing the surf away

Raindrops at the edge of eyelashes

Hail at the sound of a flash

Broken Valentine's

Steady, steady, heartbeat stutters,

When I hear your name

Pitter patter, broken clatter,

My tears fall when you're away

Twisted aether, never better,

My head to start the game

Kisser, kisser, winner loser,

Love's just another maze

Shatter, shatter, silver platter,

My heart goes long to break

Field of Life

I hear the moon kiss goodnight to the stars

I see the meadows billowing in the wind

I know when the earth moves and when the ground shakes

I feel the currents flowing through the streams

I taste the clear dew off fresh leaves

I smell the cold winds swiftly through plains

I create the songs of long lost and pain

Not Like Here

I want to live in a world where things were easier than mine

Where there are dragons and quests and end-goals

Life-long friendships and true love

Where evil is black and white

Not like here, where everything is blurry

Duller and duller than life

The Show Must Go On

Curtains close and lights turned out

Everyone outside, and wandering about

Everyone out there, but me

Being as still as could be

You were up there in the spotlight

I was down there in the low

It feels like the world was not ours

I looked to you on the stage

But your eyes crossed mine

And looked to the world

You never saw me

We weren't us and I wasn't me

You weren't you when you were up there

It feels like our chances just slipped through the cracks

The curtain call came too soon

Not the end of the show, not goodbye no thank you

You, shining under the bright lights

All that was left was me

Just me waiting in the shadows

Lone Clover

I used up all my chances

I wasted all my luck

All the time we spent together

Was gone as lighting struck

Happy memories turned to dust

Curbsides overgrown

A wish to see your light once more

The lone clover on lost shore

Familiar Nights

Empty pages, white as snow

My fingers flip through the lands I know

Welcome to the place of twinkling stars

Blinking moons, and most of all,

Sunlight lars

Their dazzling shade against the sun

Moonbeams fall down one by one

Star stripes criss-cross through the sky

Maybe I can see your eyes

Love from the Start

Gentle waves lapping along the shore

Brings us back to our origins

Our early days and playtime hours

Our laughter time and midnight showers

Make-believe towers turned cities turned worlds

Imaginations fueled by our joy

Brought to us by our mothers, our starts

Forever held steadily, forever in my heart

Lonely Sprouts

A head plops out of the soil

Then it plops, right out of the ground

Wishing good seasons and weather

But never, ever, found

Dancing On Cloud Nine

When the music starts playing

You know you can't stop

You can feel the notes through the air

Merging into one with you

Your footsteps are like honey

Smooth and youthful soul

And I just want to know

How you feel those melodies

How you create those worlds of me

The Sailor

Paddle hits the water as you're pushed out to sea

Wind in head and heart in me

The Siren

One peek above the surface

Just one little peek

What mortals see me, let them watch

Let them gape and let them taunt

Or regard me and squint

Delight in my appearance

Or timely or day

Welcome to my homely sea

The Blessed

Leather on leather

Rain on rain

The feel of the rage inside your brain

Long for the fight

Reach for the light

Ready for the fields that have your right

Spring Days

When dawn rises on the first day of spring

All I can think of is you

When bike rides were plentiful

And stargazing too

Paper planes under sunset skies

Filled the night with smiles

Lemonade filled to the brim

Catching cherry blossoms as they fell

Sneakers laid over green grass

Conversing under the shades of trees

Listening to the songs birds sing

That's the moments we live for

Passing like sidewalk chalk

Colorful and capricious

Washed away by crisp spring rains

Everlasting Guides

In a glimpse

I saw dreams

A pit of black in my head

But the pink seeped back instead

It's vibrant hues and purple tinges

The effortless clouds that floated freely

C'était les nuages qui m'ont guidé

The way the clouds float and trace the sky

To show me the way, to teach me to fly

Flourish

When you place your palms on the ground

Don't they feel warm and found

The grounded feeling you must get

When your world is surrounded by trees

Lush green life and trickling streams

Clear fresh air and mountaintop peaks

High grass and unkept greenery

Everywhere nature is key

Face it, everyone loves being free

Feel it, bend it, tumbling breeze

Always come back to me

Love in My Fingertips

Our hands were woven across the threshold as the world
changed around us
I knew I could always rely on them to be there, the
reassuring roughness against my skin
All the creases I've observed for hours on end, navigating
its mazes and scars
Opening doors to past lives, then future hopes and dreams
How each one of these etches meant something to him
And maybe one of them was there for me
I never thought about how much they conveyed love to me,
Simple digits at the edge of our bodies, at the edge of my
mind
But they held me closer, they brought me comfort, they
belonged to someone I loved
Every night without them I imagine still
Encircling my waist to hold me dear and safe
They cared for my thoughts, feelings,
They brushed away all my tears and told me it would get
better

That I could grow from all my pain

A promise that I could shed the skin of the things that

torment me, day and night

It offered new insights and gave me the choice to choose

the things I wanted in life.

For me, nothing was more beautiful than the way they

danced over railings, over my shoulder, across the table

To run over and greet my palms again in a love-radiating

embrace

And how they would clutch my hands in their own, because

they believed me,

They understood and gave me their all

Because he was there to guide them, I could see light

beyond the clouds

So maybe it was never about his hands at all, but the bright

shining light inside

The one I could find even if the mist clouded and fog

drooped over my eyes

One I would go back to again and again

Deep Blue Thoughts

Just how vast it is out there

Deep and swirling blue

Hands graze over river tops

Stretching to the sea

Oceans, rivers, all around

The water's connected to me

Graffiti

The bathroom stalls are full of them

The blacks and blues and greens

The pens the pencils that scratch the walls

Etched on poetry and jokes for all

Arguments, messages, self care reminders

Friendships ending and beginning

But come the new year, a fresh coat of paint is on

The erased marks of a pencil and pen

Just smears covered with white paint

We stare at that absence of life

Instead of the vivid colors

We forget what we had seen

We're a washed clean slate

Ready to be changed

The Sky

I love the sky,

Because the sky makes the world feel so large

I love the sky,

Because it makes the clouds that give spring rain

I love the sky,

Because its winds and warmth blows kindly through

I love the sky,

Because that's the pathway to a feeling to fly

True Peace

One step off the boat

And the world envelopes me

Clear waters, crystal springs

Mountains stretching to the sky

The true ambience of peace

Skipping Stones

Water trickles throw the still creek

The morning mist still floating midair

The smells of last night's rain

The rock that learns to fly

To feel grounded and free at the same time

Seven Lights of My Life

You've come on the rainiest of days

The darkest of nights

To dry the tears and end the fights

You tuned out the madness, and got me through

You took me on the journey of my life

Every moment I spent with you

Set my soul free

Every step and every lyric

Let me close my eyes

And take a deep breath

To appreciate my days

And when I looked up

I too, was free

Our Purple Sky

And when I was free

I looked way back

Back through both our histories

How I found you,

How you knew

That I could be here too

So when we let the balloon go

We watched it spiral up above

All of us together

Futures hand in hand

Youthful days and purple skies

Maybe, we could fly

Liberty

Traveling through thousands of cobbled streets

Breathing in the fresh air

Photographs with lens flares

The cool breeze that envelopes the warmth

And the sun that shines above

A clear blue sky with traces of clouds

To whisk me away into dreamland

For promenades and sweet birdsong

Open air music and games of toss

I take in a breath and it fills me whole

I think that I've had this feeling before

It's this feeling, airy and light

Opening, warm, and everything right

This is what being free feels like

The Sunsets We Miss

I dream about all the sunsets I'll miss

How every day passes so quickly I can barely catch a

glimpse

I wish time could just slow and life would just settle

I hope one day being alive will be enough

That I'll be able to sit there at the edge

At my balcony, at my window, on my mountains

And look out into the brisk world that's cold and free

To gaze at the watercolor that paints the skies

To stare off into clouds forevermore

songs by the sea

take in that deep breath,

what do you smell?

the sea at your fingertips

stories waiting to tell

seashells at your feet

crabs scurrying, busy

but the waves are merely beauty

the serene landscape still

To Feel Free

I want to have that magical moment

Where the main character in movies,

Is surrounded by their friends

And suddenly their world clears

And suddenly all they can see is just blue

There's no more grey clouds

And no more silver linings

Only bright days ahead

Sunlight filtering through oak trees

Boxy smiles and campfire light

Catching fireflies guided by the night

Freedom calling, freedom grows

Just one spark set to fly

Into the endless, dark sky

TAG Poem

With a click of a button we're transported to space

The land of spaghetti hair and strife

Introductions are fun, endings are sad

Pouring over art submissions

And that's how we do that

Tag parties are awesome and we're all on top

Thinking of ideas, they never stop

Book buys are the collection of all the best people

Saying hi biweekly has become our staple

Running jokes in the chat are supreme

We love all our convos and hold them dear

Because TAG is what we're all about

A gathering of people who love libraries and books

Somewhere to call home, through our little windows of

time

Neighborhood Streets

Whether it's gray skies or sunny streets

I can hear our footsteps on the gravel

The light breeze that plays with our sleeves

Curling around our ankles and down the road

Bringing a playful clearness to our lungs

And a certain excitement to our skin

They All Pop

Like bubbles floating up into the sky

It seems wherever they go I fly

Every dream that reaches the top

Ten thousand more don't seem to stop

All around they start to pop

My Secret Garden

I'm a little stone statue with cupped hands

Surrounded by miles and miles of hedge

Flowering ivy and sprouting roses

Welcome to my secret garden

There's moss that grows on my shoulders,

Providing me with warmth

And small critters that offer me company

Butterflies that fly in my heart

Clear spring water pours down my arms,

And I kiss winter goodbye

Where once was ice is now a pond

With frolicking tadpoles and lilies to hop

Toadstools to climb and tree hollows to nest

Everything flutters with sweet delight

The wooden swing hangs onto my branches

Bringing with every blossom a joy

A welcome with open arms, into the warmth

Everywhere sunbeams shine into my garden

Nibble a biscuit, stay a while

Relax a bit, enjoy your tea

Unlock and lock me at your command

Cross the threshold and under the arch

You're always welcomed here

If birds chirp at the entrance, and you see a glimmer

You're always safe and sound

Enter the garden, everything you've found

Explore our nooks, snuggle close

Lay down on our greens and free your toes

Go on barefoot upon our grounds

Feel the prickly dew and soft petals

As you walk on pass

Pick a flower, stroke a stone

Trace your initials in the stream

Watch as the ripples run away,

Then come back one by one

Learn what it's like to be me

Relish in the freedom of my garden

Stay as long as you need

the fields and forests

the breeze blows through the grasses,

swivels through the trees

your fingertips brush the past

and you long for stories deep

The Paths I Took

Brushing past tall weeds

Footsteps on the beaten grass

Path my heart leads me

Troubled Seas

My heart cast out to sea

Howling one last plea

How much you meant to me

Can you truly not see?

As the waves rock the ship

The sirens call and sing

For their only king of creed

Now read my warning- heed!

Captured Sunlight

If I captured sunlight in my fingertips

And I could paint the sky

I could count the constellations

And still have time to buy

To Be on the High Seas

Oh to be free as a pirate

Riding the high seas

Scouring the world for its secrets

Knowing no bounds as the water stretches

And reaches into every corner of this world

To feel the spray in my face

To be the wood beneath my feet change

To fall into the depths of the ocean

To feel the water through my fingers

To find the fleeting moments of rain and clouds

To bask the sun, to grasp the sand

For its lonely nights out on deck

To feel the cold blade at my neck

To fear nothing, not even death

the forgotten kingdom

Rise and rise again like dragons

Your fury burning bright

You soar and roar across your lands

So maybe your legend will live on

Dainty crowns or hard on heads

The regent's scepters will be set

The Crown

The clouds parted in the sky

Sunlight flooding the gray

The sword set in stone

Center of the world

The crowd amassed in thousands

Golden-armor clad

Waiting for the moment when

The ground moves beneath them fast

Then the sun hits the earth

And all becomes still

For it's time to bow before the new leader

Long live the queen

Let there be Dragons

When the wind blows north

Strong and cold

Let there be dragons

Long and old

Light the flames

And melt the ice

Make the stories come from told

Bend the hours day by day

Wrath in your glory

Dragon's bane

Color Scheme

I picked the green shirt on the pile

Intended to put it on

"No!" Said the lady pushing me away,

"Pick red, it's the color today!"

They didn't know that I wanted green to stay

But on was the red shirt here on my head

"Green is for envy and nasty nature. Red is sure to bring

you pleasure!"

"Red brings attention and luck and love, who wouldn't

want this red?"

I nodded because why wouldn't I want these things?

Attention and love and luck and happiness?

So I bought the red shirt to feel so happy

But I look in the mirror and I see nobody

A Life With the Windows Open

And if life could slow down just one bit

I could open the windows and doors

To embrace the warm wind that flows through the

openings

That swirl and dance in my room

I could live my life without obligations

Freedom to do what I love

To explore, and learn, and cherish my days

Because I know that for sure

All that I love is what I have passed

I spent every waking minute

And every hour I slept

Was spent according to my will

Serenity

My subtle fingers open the doors

Peaceful museum scenery

Serene, quiet, beauty

Paintings made so long ago

Waiting for me to find

Colourful days, sleepless nights

Forest greens and city lights

Loopy cursive handwriting

Writing without skill

How I wish I could be in one

Peaceful paintings still

loveless

on loveless nights, I reach out for your hand

the flowers wilted on the sill

the locket around my neck so heavy

i walk by the riverside to forget your name

but like the current which flows to the lake

you always come back to me the same

Raindrops on My Window

Every memory feels so fleeting

Fast and swift across my eyes,

Like the raindrops on my window

As the car speeds ahead

I can't see the road clearly

Or the sidewalk on the side

All I see is gray and clouds

Is this what life's become?

I'm present but my mind is flying

Everything fades into a blur

Against the background days

Years merge into the past

And for once, I can't remember

I can't recall a single one

gray clouds

gray skies turn into gray lies

flowers all strewn on the tiles

marble flooring and shining walls

wisps that float through the night

memories, mind, maybe mine

how could you forget and be so fine?

The Passage of Time

When the clouds move above me

All that I see is still

The world around me spins

Just a river around a rock

Will you be around to see,

The darkness falling, spilling on the streets?

Strange things lurking, just behind the trees?

The leaves drifting onto the dirt road,

The mittens on the ground,

Or letters sent to me?

Creatures

Deep in the forest where creatures dwell

Dark ones and light ones

Scary ones and gentle ones

Meek ones and daring ones

It's those that really count

The few that actually shout

For a scream in the darkness

Means absolutely nothing

I Wish For

Over the valleys and through the bones

Seeking through stories I can't withhold

Finding the truth

Marking the walls

Watch as the fire burns everything out

Flow with the rain

Go with the drought

What's controlling nature making it go about

Over the hills and under the trees

Whimsical for days that weren't meant to be

Someone Other Than Me

It's spooky and funny and there's candy around

There's costumes, friends, and haunted houses,

And I love Halloween for that too

But there's more to it than just that

The masks, the wardrobe, the things we say

On Halloween I can be someone I want to see

The one day of the year where I can be

Someone other than me

Truly Mischievous

Ha ha,

You think you're clever when you say

Solved the murder moved on away

You saw me there then here again

I will always be your friend

Creeping down the corridors

Lurking round the cracks

Knocking, breaking, crashing sounds

Who knows how I could be found?

I pile, I hide, I burn and I cry

Who can find me,

Can you try?

Nice one,

Truly Mischievous

From the Outside In

My life feels like those movies

Where the character walks down the street

And left and right and all they see

Are warm homes and warm families

And every time I peer in, nobody sees me

I'm just alone in the cold in the shadows

Looking from the outside in

And I'd bang on the doors but that'd disturb the peace

And I can't disturb that warmth, the happiness

Because I am but a cold and lonely thing

Looking from the outside in

the darkest of days

the door swings open, floorboard creaks

oh my, what secrets, do you keep?

up the winding staircase and into the halls

dark paintings peering down

another door opens, without a sound

the wind blows west from here

the candlelight flickers out

Pictures in their Frames

I turn off the light and the pictures look dark in their
frames
Devoid of color, of art, and life
Black shadows reminiscent to a glorious past
Now cast away behind the attic glass

Thinking in the Dark

Sometimes it's better to think in the dark
When it's just you and your brain
Without the colors and without the world
There's no light to disturb your sight

Abandoned Life

Rose petals fall in an abandoned mansion

Stories and secrets long forgotten

So let the whispers melt into the mist

And let the moors sleep still

Wings

Pain always works in the long run

Hope is always fickle

I will never get over it,

But my happiness is simple

Where do my thoughts go,

Out into space

Darkness marks my hands now

Light fades away

Maybe I should embrace these wings

Night without the day

Across the Water

Streaks across the water

Waves upon waves

Longing for a waiting graze

For what seems like a bother

Is not both or neither

But what lies inside the cold, unopened gaze

Pigeon

City streets are filled with people

But the benches sit wide and free

Gray clouds above and street signs

Here the sun cannot shine

Welcome to the land of grief

Where my wings had spread too soon

My freedom bought by guilt

Before my memory brought me doom

The City

City streets and neon lights

Crosswalk lanes and midnight sights

Flashing lights and nighttime shock

Give or take and fake it all

Who cares if you fall?

Not them, not the others

Watching as you shout

Help me, help me

Silenced pleas

Screaming all drowned out

The Thin Red Line

The thin red line where heroes fly

Off to the distance and into the sky

Into the heaven of hell where angels die

The thin pink line stepped and torn

Faded and worn

With worry but forlorn

Separated but by a thread

So broken yet so fractured

On the surface of the moon

Here we have heroes

Gray

Darkness becomes darker

Light becomes lighter

But gray will always stay gray

Where I Write

Pencil scratches against porcelain

Pen taps against inkwells

Who's to say, where you write

In your head, in your heart, in your mind?

This Chair

In the corner there sits a chair

Roughed edges and worn wood

Deep creases and rigid corners

Its burnt legs blackened

One sits there and ponders, wonders

Thinks and grieves

What had this chair seen?

The weary warriors that sat

The kings and queens before that

Their reasons and stories with this chair

Every knife mark carved

Every dark cloak draped

The lone man starved

As the one earth shakes

Or the young petit couple

Who aren't seeing double

A loveseat this could be

Or a cradle of eternity

Where the old lady knits on Sundays

Where I tie my shoe at the end of a long fray

The chair that's climbed on for a better view

The chair that's turned to cue

Kicked over in frustration

Smashed in anger

Thrown on when in grief

Tilted back in joy

But then again, it could be

Just a chair

Hearty Soup

Hearty soups come from here

The soul and feelings of one fair

One did not know

Such atmosphere could exist

In such a beauty

Of a food from the heart

Winter Under the Fir Trees

A peek under the lush branches and they reveal

A world of magic and all things real

The glimmer of snow underneath the sun

Carpeting the world in a wintery glow

The frost that lingers on the branches of trees

And the snow that drifts with the wind

Brings with it carriages and snow angels

And long built snowmen that stand on guard

Lopsided and wonky snowballs that are piled up high

Colourful snow gear that contrast the ice

Laughter and cheer as the streets come alight

And with the warm drinks between mittened hands

We can grin at the sky and the twinkling stars above

The aroma of baked goods that waft into our noses

Maybe it's the beginnings of a winter fantasy

One that can last forever, one that can stay endlessly

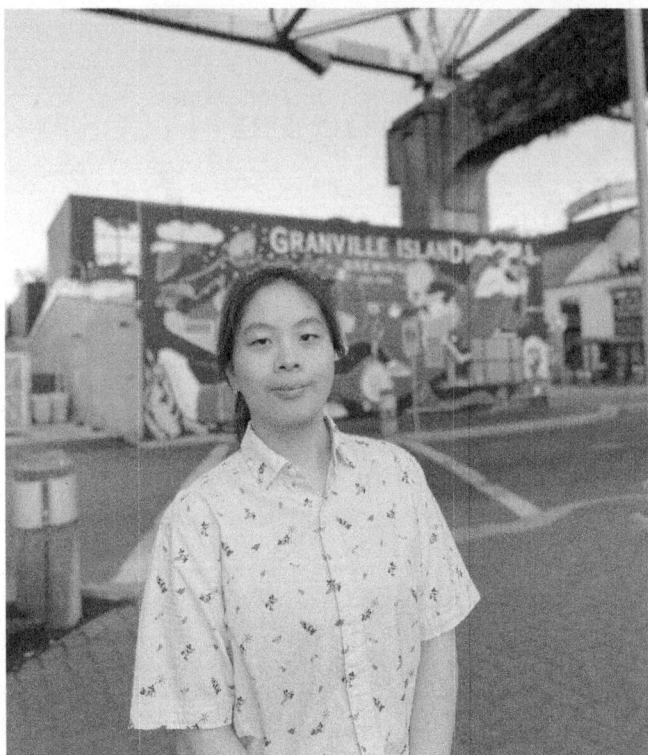

About the Author

Milian RJ Chen loves and cherishes a myriad of hobbies and passions, from writing and learning about animals to watercolour painting and watching movies. She's loved writing (and reading) from a young age, publishing her first real book shortly after her seventeenth birthday.

You can find her on social media at @chen.milian and @the_turquoise_quill on Instagram.

milianchen.com

Journey through the
pages and find poems
that resonate with you.

Made in the USA
Las Vegas, NV
20 November 2023